Crisis In Crimea

A Historical Lead Up To The Conflict Between Russia And Ukraine

Table of Contents

Introduction

This year, the world has witnessed the growing volatility of Ukraine's governmental landscape. Ukraine is a country situated between Europe and Federal Russia and is considered the "breadbasket" of Europe. It was one of the original constituents of the Soviet Union that dissolved in 1991. Since then, it has established a rather unstable democracy with a very frail economy.

Within the country today, an acute political rift emerged between its pro-Russian eastern and its pro-Europe western regions. This all began when Ukraine's pro-Russia President Viktor Yanukovych declined an association agreement with the European Union. The agreement aimed at the integration of Ukrainian economy with the Western countries, which many Ukrainians saw as their chance for economic prosperity. Due to Yanukovych's rejection of the deal, mass upheavals started to ensue across Ukraine and the once internal unrest careened towards a war with its powerful neighbor, Russia. Fights broke between Ukraine patriots and Russian military troops sided by pro-Russia Ukrainian rebels. Russia's aggression quickly led to international involvement in which world leaders urged the two nations to arrive at a diplomatic solution. According to them the problem has great possibility of reaching a global scale if not addressed promptly.

Any evaluation of the possible outcomes of this conflict and the implications of such outcomes require one to understand its root causes. Many of the factors boil down to Russia's centuries-long dominion over Ukraine. So why is Ukraine so important to Russia? Why do some regions of Ukraine identify themselves intrinsically linked to Russia while some side with Europe? Where is the Crimean Peninsula and who is its lawful owner? To answer these questions and understand the intricacies of their answers, this book will bring you back to history. Witness how the relationship of these two nations unfolded and how they connect to present events.

Chapter 1 - Kievan Rus': The predecessor of Russia and Ukraine

Kiev, the modern capital of Ukraine, is usually denoted as the cradle of Rus' civilization or the mother of Russian cities. Modern peoples of Russia, Ukraine and Belarus all assert that Keivan Rus' is their cultural inheritance. The once great Keivan Rus' state was a loose East Slavic federation in Europe. "Rus" is the Slavic word for the red-haired Scandinavian warriors—the Vikings— who founded this medieval empire after gaining entry from the North. Under the rule of Rurik dynasty, the Vikings conquered the local Slavic tribes from the late 9th to the mid-13th century.

In the 9th century, Prince Oleg became the first ruler of the Kievan Rus' and expanded his dominion to the Novgorod south alongside the river valley of Dnieper. He defended trade from the intrusion of Khazars from the east, and he moved the state's capital to the more strategic Kiev. The first major territorial expansion of the Kievan Rus' was achieved by Sviatoslav I after combatting against Khazar Empire in a war of conquest.

In 988, Vladimir the Great started Easter Orthodox Christianity in the Rus' state through his own conversion, which laid the foundation of the modern Russian church. Vladimir the Great passed a decree that converted all the people of Kiev to being Christians. At its peak expansion in the mid-11th century under the rule of Yaroslav I (1019–1054), Rus' united the majority of East Slavic tribes as it stretched northward to the Baltic Sea, southward to the Black Sea, westward to the headwaters of Vistula and eastward to the Taman Peninsula. Shortly after the death of Yaroslav, his sons authored and circulated the Rus' Justice, which was the first written legal code of the state.

In the late 11th century until the 12th century, the decline of Keivan Rus' began. Economic issues such as the breakdown of Rus'-Byzantium commercial ties (due to the weakening of Constantinople), accompanied by the reduction of trade routes through the state caused the division of Rus' into several conflicting regional powers. In the early 12th century, Halych (Galicia), The Kiev, Volodymyr (Vladimir-Volhynia), Chernigov, Podolia, and other independent regions arose in Southwest Rus. Toward the end of the 12th century, the Halych-Volhynian region emerged. In 1240s, Mongols of the Golden Horde invaded and finally dissolved Kievan Rus'.

Chapter 2 - Ukraine under the Russian Empire and the Polish-Lithuanian Commonwealth

The Mongol's conquest over Kievan Rus' resulted in the divergence of the histories of Russian and Ukrainian people.http://en.wikipedia.org/wiki/Russia%E2%80%93Ukraine _relations - cite_note-Gumelev-9 Russians created the powerful Russian state after effectively uniting the fragments of the northern provinces of Rus'. The Ukrainians, on the other hand, were dominated by the Grand Duchy of Lithuania, and in 1386 the Polish-Lithuanian Commonwealth was established. The union of Poland and Lithuanian dynasties enabled the Polish to expand to Ukraine, while Ukraine prospered under Lithuanian. Meanwhile in 1478, the Ottoman Empire absorbed the Black Sea shore governed by Crimean khans.

Due to the political, cultural and demographic, pressure of polonization (the imposition or acquisition of Polish culture) many landowning nobilities of Polish Ruthenia (alternative title for the land of Rus') converted to Catholicism and became indistinguishable from Polish nobility. Meanwhile, the Orthodox Church of Ukraine suffered persecution. Due to the confrontation of Polish Catholicism, the Ukrainian Orthodox bishops founded the Uniate (Greek Catholic) faith in 1596. The church acknowledged the authority of the pope but remained steadfast to the Orthodox rite.

In the 15th century, no interstate relations occurred between Northeast Rus (the Russian state) and Lithuania (which ruled Ukraine). Several contacts occurred, however, but they are mostly bonds of kinship between the princes as well as civil tug-of-war between Lithuanian parties and princes aiming for foreign political gains.

In the 16th century, the term Ukraine, meaning "borderland" or "at the border" started to become widely used. During that time, the emerging principality of Muscovy (present day Moscow) and the Poland-Lithuanian Commonwealth were contesting for authority over this huge region south of their borderlines. The hostile circumstances under the Polish rule urged many Ukrainians to flee polonization and religious persecution by relocating to the thinly populated steppes of Central Ukraine below the Dnieper rapids (also identified as the Wild Fields). There, they founded a militant order named the Zaporizhzhya Sich (or literally translated as "clearing beyond the rapids"). These fugitives later became recognized as Kozaks or Cossacks, which is an adaptation of kazak, a Turkic word meaning "adventurer" or "outlaw." The commoners—townspeople and peasants—deprived of native protection once offered by the Rus' nobility, began seeking for security from the Zaporozhian Cossacks. The group became a well-respected entity with its own parliamentary system of government. It became a strong political and military force that challenged the authority of the Polish–Lithuanian Commonwealth as they strongly declined polonization.

In 1648-1654, the struggle of Ukrainians against Polish-Lithuanian Commonwealth occupation began.

Ukrainians and Belarusians, led by Cossack Hetmanate Bohdan Khmelnitsky, successfully waged a liberation war against the government. Since Ukraine was too frail to stand alone, it sought alliance from the three powers. The negotiation with the principality of Muscovy– with which they share a large portion of their culture, religion and language— was the most successful of all. The absorption of Ukraine into the Russian Empire was legalized by the Treaty of Pereyaslav in 1654. The union was completed in the late 18th century (with the Partitions of Poland). Meanwhile, the land on the left bank of the Dnieper river valley, the Hetmanate, was granted independence within Russia.

The Cossacks gained support from Russian troops due to the Treaty of Pereyaslav. Its fundamental provisions stated that Ukraine was to be mainly independent. The Ukrainian lands within the Kiev, Chernigov and Poltava provinces, as well as majority of Podolia and Volhynia, should join Muscovy under the title "Smaller Russia." The lands were bound to offer Russia alliance during wartime, an in return the Tsar pledged protection for Ukraine against aggressions. The Russians soon started to infringe Ukraine's rights that the czars derisively denoted the Ukrainians as "Little Russians," as opposed to the "Great Russians" of the Russian realm. Although old and contemporary historians have varying opinions about the treaty, it is generally agreed on that the Treaty of Pereyaslav set the first legal partition between the Polish-Lithuanian Commonwealth and Ukraine, and that Russia acknowledged Ukraine as an autonomous body.

In 1658-1659, the Hetmans from the right-bank Ukraine tried to gain independence from the Muscovite influence through a treaty with Poland in 1658. However, when the Russo-Polish war ended with the Treaty of Andrusovo of 1667 and the Eternal Peace Treaty of 1686, Russia and the Polish Commonwealth divided Ukraine between themselves. Russia acquired east of the Dnieper River, Kiev, and left-bank (or East) Ukraine while Poland retained control over right-bank (or West) Ukraine.

Hetman Ivan Mazepa, ruling over a weakened Cossack state, attempted once again to break Ukraine free from Russian domination. While Russia was at war with King Charles XII of Sweden during the Great Northern War, Mazepa went over to the side of Sweden. Mazepa expected that the quasi-regular Cossack troops or what is known as the "register Cossacks" would support him due to the swelling discontent with Muscovy. Conversely, Mazepa received no backing from the Cossacks and the rest of Ukraine. Their defeat at Poltava by Czar Peter I (1709) crushed the last hopes of Mazepa to hand Ukraine over from Muscovy to Sweden. This further restrained Ukrainian autonomy.

In the second half of the 18th century, South Ukraine gained independence from the Ottoman rule. At the end of the century, Russia unified Ukrainian lands along the right bank of the Dnieper. The Russian Empire gave Ukraine great autonomy for the most part of the 18th century and Kirill Razumovsky was its last Hetman.

However, due to its series of conflicts and alliances with the three powers, the Cossack host was forcibly disbanded by the Russian Empire. In 1764, a decree abolishing the Hetmanate was issued by Empress Catherine the Great. In 1775, the abolition of Zaporozhian host followed. Majority of their population moved to the Kuban region, the southernmost part of the Russian Empire. In that area, the Cossacks played a major role in protecting the Empire against the ferocious Caucasian tribes and in return, the Tsars gave them a great degree of freedom.

Ukraine, with the termination of its greater political autonomy, was eventually divided into three provinces. In accordance to the Polish partition treaties of 1772, 1793 and 1795, Austria seized Galicia, while The Russian Empire seized the entirety of Ukraine in the right banks of Dnieper (Podolia and Volhynia). This consequently reunified right-bank and left-bank Ukraine. The left bank of the Dnieper was named Small Russia while the right bank as Southwest Province, and South Ukraine was known as Nova Rossia. After the Russo-Turkish War of 1768-1774, the Crimean Khanate gained independence from all foreign influence; however, it was integrated to Russia in 1783.

The civil administration and the army safeguarded the Russian influence over Ukraine during the reign of Alexander (1801-1825). In the 1830s, a centralized Russian government under the leadership of Nicholas I (1825-1855) controlled the entire Ukraine that even the usage of the name "Ukraine" ceased at that period. The Russian government began to ban the usage of the Ukrainian language in publications and in schools. This resulted to an emergence of a Ukrainian movement in the late 19th century that encourages the revival of its national and cultural heritage. Meanwhile, there was also renewed commotion for Ukrainian liberation and for the unity of all lands of Ukraine under a single state (including the Austria-Hungary–Galicia, Ruthenia and Bukovina). After emerging as a political nationality in the 1848 Austrian Revolution, the Galician Ukrainians made Galicia a harbour for Russian Ukraine's nationalist movements. This undertaking was headed by underground educational groups called hromadas which the czar constantly suppressed.

During the Revolution of 1905, the Russian authority was eventually obligated to lift the veto on publications using the Ukrainian language. This also resulted in the establishment of the Prosvit public education societies. In the Russia's Federal Assembly, the State Duma was established and granted limited legislative powers following the tsar's manifesto of 30 October 1905. The members of the Duma were selected through the curial electoral system. During the election, the Ukrainians were given the right to choose their own representatives to the first and second dumas. Among the representatives elected were patriotic Ukrainian leaders as well as commoners (peasants). A Ukrainian committee consisting of 44 members were members of the First Duma (10 May–21 July 1906) while 47 members existed in the Second Duma (5 March–15 June 1907). They eventually created the Ukrainian Duma Hromada which had its independent political program.

Chapter 3 - The First World War

When the First World War ensued on 1914-1919, about 3 million Ukrainians served the Russian armies. Meanwhile, more than 250,000 fought in the Austrian forces. Ukraine suffered immediate devastation as it was caught between the major contending nations. On the eastern front, the war in Galicia was one of the greatest battles. A large proportion of Western Ukraine was terribly affected by repeated attacks and occupation. Before the war broke, West Ukraine sought alliance with the Hapsburg dynasty. As the war began, they then founded an umbrella organization called the Supreme Ukrainian Council in Lviv. They assembled a volunteer legion known as the Ukrainian Sich Riflemen which comprised 2,500 men. It became the first modern-time Ukrainian military unit. In Vienna, they formed a coordinating body known as the General Ukrainian Council comprising of 7 Bukovynian and 21 Galician representatives as well as 3 affiliates of the Union for the Liberation of Ukraine. The union are Russian-ruled Ukraine expatriates who asked support from the Austrian and German for the foundation of an independent Ukrainian state.

In September, 1914, much of Galicia and Bukovyna had been occupied by Russian troops. The retreating authorities of Hapsburg arrested and executed hundreds of suspected pro-Russian Ukrainians without trial. They then deported more than 30,000 Ukrainians (including several Russophiles) to internment camps such as the one near Thalerhof in Austria. Meanwhile, the West Ukrainians who were under Russian occupation also suffered extremely harsh treatment. Thousands of Ukrainian activists had been arrested and deported by the Russian authorities to prevent difficulties in russifying the population. Ukrainian institutions were also shut down and the use of Ukrainian language was banned again. In addition, they launched a movement to dissolve the Greek Catholic church, extraditing Metropolitan Andrei Sheptytsky to Russia in the process. Once again, Austria occupied West Ukraine in 1915 while Ukrainian activities in the rest of Ukraine were completely repressed until the rising of the Revolution of 1917.

Chapter 4 - Ukraine's Struggle for Independence

Diplomatic, military and political activities emerged between 1917 and 1920 to attain Ukrainian statehood in all Ukrainian territories. At first, this movement focuses on the central Ukrainian regions, which were under the control of the Russian authorities until 1917. After the February Revolution of 1917, central Ukraine established three Ukrainian state formations.

The February Revolution of 1917

Following the First World War, public dissatisfaction, an economic crisis and military failure debilitated the Russian Empire. The oppressed nationalities sought independence, the peasants demanded more land, and the working class wanted improvements on their work and home environments. In short, almost every sector of the society wanted to break free from the domination of the Central Powers. As a result, a second revolution (subsequent to the Revolution of 1905) emerged within the Empire. This resulted to the dissolution of the tsarist regime and the establishment of Russian Soviet Federative Socialist Republic (Russian SFSR)— a democratic, republican government.

Social disorder, army damages and chaos immediately resulted to inadequate food supply in Petrograd. This subsequently caused labours of the Putilov factory to strike on March 2, 1917 and for workers all over Petrograd to go on strike as well. On March 12, the soldiers joined the labours. The soldiers were guard troops that held many Ukrainians, such as the Volhynian Regiment. The regiment was associated with the Ukrainian Social Democrats and with Volodymyr Vynnychenko, a well-known Ukrainian activist. That day, the State Duma, under the command of Mikhailo Hrushvesky, assumed power over Russia and created the Provisional Committee to head the rebellion. The committee was supervised by liberal zemstvo leader Prince G. Lvov. Other members include the Octobrists (A. Guchkov), Kadets (Pavel Miliukov), Social Democrats (N. Chkheidze), Socialist Revolutionaries (Aleksandr Kerensky), and independent supporters (M. Tereshchenko and others). The Bolshevik, a Russian faction, opposed the Provisional Government. However, due to the Government's influence over an increasing number of labourers' and soldiers' deputies, they succeeded in forming a state with two authorities.

On March 15, Tsar Nicholas II was renounced, and the Provisional Government designated its own gubernial and county officials all over the empire—including Ukraine—after ousting the tsar's high commissioners (governors). During the rebellion, the Ukrainians structured their own body of representatives—the Ukrainian National Council in Petrograd. Oleksander Lototsky became the council head and asked the Provisional Government for Ukraine state rights. Another Ukrainian party led by Oleksander Shulhyn was created in the Petrograd Soviet of Workers' and Soldiers' Deputies.

The revolt rapidly spread through the entire Russian Empire. It was considered a social rebellion on Russian ethnic lands and a national rebellion on non-Russian lands. Meanwhile, the Ukrainians formed their own groups claiming language recognition, separate military groups, and Ukrainian schools. The language ban as previously implemented by the tsarist authority slowly lost its power. The Ukrainian language was slowly used in administration, the academe, in the media and publishing. The Central Rada, a Ukrainian central council, was established in Kviv to head the national movement of Ukrainians. Mykhailo Hrushevsky presided over the Central Rada, while Vladimir Vinnichenko was designated as premier and Simon Petlura as war minister. The Russian Provisional Government's power over Ukraine eventually ceased, and its roles were then performed by the Central Rada.

On April 19-21 1917, the Rada became the revolutionary parliament of Ukraine after the convention in the All-Ukrainian National Congress. This period was marked by the emergence of several Ukrainian civic, cultural as well as political parties: these include the Ukrainian Party of Socialist Revolutionaries, Ukrainian Social Democratic Workers' party, Ukrainian Party of Socialists-Federalists, Ukrainian

Democratic Agrarian party, Ukrainian Party of Socialists-Independents, among others. Several professional unions and associations also became dynamic activists and sent representatives to the Central Rada.

Generally, Ukraine went through the February Revolution in a more organized and peaceful way than the Russians and other oppressed nationalities. Several assemblies and protests were made without bloodshed. Aside from social transformation, the fight for cultural, political, national and political privileges contributed greatly in the Ukrainian revolt.

October Revolution of 1917

After waging a revolution in October 1917, the Bolsheviks were vanquished in Ukraine as well as in Cossack domains along the waters of Don and Kuban. The government of Ukraine then started to establish local administrations, aiming to integrate all places inhabited by indigenous Ukrainians.

In November 1917, the foundation of the Ukrainian People's Republic was declared by the Central Rada and the name was retained until November 1918. The republic was composed of the Kiev, Poltava, Yekaterinoslav, Kharkov, Chernigov, and the provinces of Tauria (Crimea) and Volhynia. The third decree of the Rada declared that Ukraine, however, would be maintaining official relations with Russian Provisional Government. Ukraine was represented by its commissar Petro Stebnytsky at the Russian government while Dmitriy Odinets was designated as the representative of Russian Affairs in the Ukrainian Republic.

Though initially proclaiming itself a republic within the structure of a federated Russia, Ukraine declared full independence and withdrawal from the Russian Republic through the fourth decree of January 25, 1918 as a result of the Soviet military aggression. Soviet troops headed to Ukraine, but since the Central Powers recognized Ukrainian independence, they sent their own soldiers to the territory to force Russia's Red Army to withdraw. In March 1918, the Treaty of Brest-Litovsk was signed separately by Russia and Ukraine to calm the military turmoil between them. The same year, peace negotiations were also initiated.

The World War I ceasefire of November 1918, in turn forced the Central Powers to withdraw relations with Ukraine. With the collapse of Austria-Hungary, a West Ukrainian independent republic had been declared in Lviv. For a brief moment, the Ukrainian National Republic (East Ukraine) and the Western Ukrainian People's Republic (Galicia) proclaimed unity in January 1919. However, shortly after the union, Soviet troops promptly occupied Kiev. A four-cornered battle occurred among Ukrainian forces, the Red Army, the insurgent army of Denikin, and the Poles.

In March 1919, the All-Ukraine Congress of Soviets that assembled in Kiev adopted the "independent Ukrainian Soviet Socialist Republic" constitution. The administration declared Soviet Ukraine and appealed military support from the Bolshevik based in Moscow. After World War I, Ukraine had been a battlefield for the Russian Civil War. Both Ukrainian and Russians combatted under nearly all armies according to their political standpoint.

The independent state of Ukraine of 1917-1920 was eventually ended by Poland and Soviet Russia, distributing Ukraine between them while a number of Ukrainian regions were unified with Romania and Czechoslovakia. Soviet Russia and Soviet Ukraine agreed on the Union Treaty of Workers and Peasants for Military and Economic Cooperation in 1920 that formalized, once again, Ukraine's subservience to Russia. As the Red Army conquered the Whites in the Crimean peninsula, Crimea was fused into the Russian Federation. Following the Treaty of Riga of 1921, West Ukraine was handed to Poland.

Chapter 5 - The Soviet Socialist Republics

On December 1922, Ukraine SSR and Russian SFSR became one of the original constituent republics of the Union of Soviet Socialist Republics (USSR) or otherwise known as the Soviet Union. Other subnational Soviet republics of the USSR include the Transcaucasian SFSR and the Byelorussian SSR.

The Soviet Union was a socialist, single-party state that existed from 1922 to 1991, and it was ruled by the Communist Party with Moscow as its capital.http://en.wikipedia.org/wiki/Soviet_Union - cite_note-3 Although, in technical terms, a federal system was constituted in the USSR, it had a highly centralized governance and economy, with significant policymaking taking place at the Kremlin. Fundamentally, the 11 constituent republics (which include Armenia, Azerbaijan, Estonia, Georgia, Kyrgyzstan, Kazakhstan, Latvia, Lithuania, Moldova, Tajikistan, Turkmenistan and Uzbekistan) were unitary states with lesser power and are direct subordinates of the founding members Russian, Ukraine, Transcaucasian and Byelorussian republics.

Under the Soviet Union, the Russian SFSR's economy underwent immense industrialization and it produced around two-thirds of USSR's electricity. Russia trailed behind the United States and Saudi Arabia as the leading producer of petroleum in the world. The republic was able to establish 475 institutions of higher education and 47 languages became the medium of instruction to some 23,941,000 students. In the health sector, regionally structured public-health facilities delivered care to the people. After 1985, however, the Gorbachev administration's restructuring rules (e.g. the establishment of enterprises not owned by the state, such as cooperative) somewhat slackened the economy. This ultimately led to economic stagnation, with early signs seen in the late 1970s. The result of such market policies made way for several enterprises to fail and for the overall economic instability by 1990.

Meanwhile, the Ukrainian SSR's administrative territory changed several times under the USSR. Regional annexations and restructuring were made during World War II. In August 1939, The Soviet Union and Germany settled the Molotov-Ribbentrop Pact or otherwise known as the Treaty of Non-Aggression. Its Secret Additional Protocol delineated the sphere of power of USSR and Germany in Eastern Europe. In September 1939, the USSR occupied Poland to extend its eastern grounds. New territories were integrated into Ukraine and six new regions were constituted. In November 1940, Bessarabia was integrated into Ukraine while the Trans-Carpathian Region followed in 1945. In 1954, the efforts of Nikita Khrushchev (CPSU Central Committee's First Secretary) resulted in the handover of Crimea to Ukraine through an executive order of the Russian Federation's Presidium of the Supreme Council.

In July 1990, Ukraine implemented the Declaration of State Sovereignty and in August 1991, the Act of Declaration of Independence. In December 1991, the newly elected President Leonid Kravchuk proclaimed that Kiev was decisively declining to agree on any kind of treaty with the Soviet Union, whether economic or political. This marked the dissolution of the USSR.

Chapter 6 - Holodomor: The Face of Soviet Famine in Ukraine (*A Special Coverage*)

In 1932 to 1932, millions of famine deaths occurred throughout the USSR due to severe food shortage in its primary grain-producing lands. Aside from eastern and southern part Ukraine, areas affected included Volga Region and Kazakhstan, Northern Caucasus, West Siberia and South Urals. At that time, the West Ukraine was spared as it was under the Polish rule (through the 1921 Treaty of Riga). The subset of the Soviet famine as it happened in Ukraine is termed as *Holodomor*, which is a Ukrainian for "extermination by hunger" or "killing by starvation". This man-made famine also known as the "Terror-Famine in Ukraine" and "Famine-Genocide in Ukraine" killed an estimated 7.5 million citizens, mostly in the eastern part of the country. This peacetime catastrophe is unprecedented by any event in the history of the Ukraine.

Scholars debate on the arbitrary significance of bad economic policies and natural factors as factors of famine. However, since 2006, this event has been known by Ukraine and more than 20 other nations as a *genocide* of the Ukrainian populace. On 13 January 2010, Kiev Appellate Court posthumously sentenced Stalin, Molotov, Kaganovich, Chubarand, Kosior and other officials of Soviet Communist Party guilty of Ukrainian genocide during the famine. In 2011, a documentary entitled Genocide Revealed presented proof for the standpoint that Stalin and the Soviet

Communist regime purposefully directed the mass starvation of 1932–1933 to Ukrainians.

Usage of the term "Holodomor"

The Ukrainian term Holodomor as literally translated to English is "death by hunger", "to starve to death", or "to kill by hunger". Sometimes the word is translated as "murder by hunger or starvation". The term can be found in prints of Ukrainian immigrant organizations in the Canada and the U. S. as early as 1978. However, even long after the de-Stalinization of the Soviet Union in 1956, mentions of the famine were carefully watched. Historians were only allowed to use the expression 'food difficulties', and using the very term holod/golod (famine/ hunger) was prohibited. It was only in the late 1980s when the use of the term Holodomor came to be more acceptable as part of the Soviet policy for increased transparency and openness, Glasnost. In December 1987, Central Committee of the Communist Party of Ukraine First Secretary Volodymyr Shcherbytskyi officially used the term Holodomor for the first time in his speech during Ukraine Republic's 70th anniversary. In February 1988, it was again mentioned in public during the speech of Oleksiy Musiyenko, an officer of the Ukraine division of the Union of Soviet Writers. in the USSR, Holodomor's first appearance in publication may have been in Musiyenko's writings on the topic. "Holodomor" is officially entered in the contemporary, two-volume Ukrainian language dictionary printed in 2004. The word is defined as "artificial hunger, organised on a vast scale by a criminal regime against a country's population."

Causes of famine

The causes of Holodomor are subject to political and scholarly debate. Even though some proposed that the man-made famine was a form of deliberate attack by Soviet leaders, the lack of irrefutable proof of intent in the earlier days made other scholars believe that Holodomor was merely an outcome of economic problems. It had been associated with drastic economic changes instigated during the time of private property bankruptcy and Soviet industrial development.

The Gold Blockade is said to be one substantial contributing factor in the economic problems of the Soviet Union, and hence the starvation. In 1925, the rejection of western countries to receive gold as medium of payment resulted in little timber, oil and grain as trade currency. In April 1993, the United Kingdom passed a law that prohibits the import of Russian goods such as petroleum, timber, wheat, barley and butter. The Soviet Union had been suffering from little trade currency other than grain until the law was revoked in July of the same year. By then, however, damage has already been done.

To address the food shortage during the Gold Blockade, Stalin established a collectivization drive assuming it would increase farm yields. However, it contributed to the 1932 famine. Even though Ukraine was in no risk of climatic famine in 1932, because of a median grain yield of around 147 million centers (which was about 16 million centers greater than in 1928), collectivization caused starvation in rural populations. Some 110,000 special Bolshevik agents were sent to Ukraine's rural areas to conduct forced grain collection over both independent and collectivized farmers. In order to curtail numerous peasant revolts that ensued, a law was proclaimed in August 1932 introducing death penalty to those who violate the rules of grain collection.

Following the First Five-Year Plan, fewer lands were seeded than intended and instead of familiar crops; unfamiliar ones such as cotton and sugar beets were grown in Ukrainian farms. Consequently, people in rural areas were left with no means of food sustenance. The lack of significant management of supplies by the Soviet authority exacerbated the situation. Even though there was a great amount of harvested grain, huge losses occurred during processing, transportation, or storage.

Genocide by the Soviet regime

There is argument as to the extent of Joseph Stalin's premeditated act to destroy the peasantry of Ukraine. However, using the term of Holodomor to refer to the starvation highlights its man-made facets. Scholars argue that it is intended—thus an act of genocide—to reject outside aid and seize all household foodstuffs. In addition, the event would fall under the lawful meaning of genocide due to Soviet actions and policies aiming to curb the emergence of Ukrainian patriotism. There have been particularly harmful rules that were proclaimed in and mainly limited to Soviet Ukraine from 1932-1933.

It is said that the main goal of the genocide was to dissolve the pillars of the Ukrainian state through the destruction of the kulak class. The kulaks include the whole peasantry (together with those joining collectivism), which the Bolshevik government considered as the bulk of Ukraine's patriots who fought for their liberation during the Russian Revolution. Massive crusades led by P. Postyshev were initiated in an attempt to subdue the Ukrainian culture. Postyshev was the CC CP(B)U's second secretary sent by Stalin from Moscow. However, chief members of the CP(B)U which include Mykola Skrypnyk, Hryhorii Petrovsk and Vlas Chubar attempted to convince their president, Postyshev, as well as their allies to initiate policy reforms that could impede the progress of the famine. Their exertions were refused by Stalin and they were even indicted of sabotage. In their great opposition to the pervasive killing, Mykola Khvylovy and Skrypnyk committed suicide.

Duration and scope of famine

As early as 1930, advisers and academics predicted the occurrence of famine in the Ukrainian state but few to no preventive measures were taken. In the spring of 1933 and from February to July of the same year, the famine struck Ukrainian SSR, including the Moldavian Autonomous SSR (a region of Ukrainian SSR that time). The highest number of casualties was documented in the spring of 1933. In 1932, only around 4 million tons of harvest was obtained by Soviet authorities, as compared to approximately 7 million tons procured from the harvest in 1931. Town rations were radically reduced and in 1932-1933 winters and 1933 spring, many citizens of the urban regions starved.

The famine affected almost all the regions of interwar Soviet Ukraine, but massive proportions grew in the areas of eastern and southern oblasts. Neighbouring territories of the republic which were mostly populated by Ukrainians (e.g. the Don region and the Kuban) were also affected. However, the privileged Communist functionaries in the rural areas, which were an insignificant portion of the population, did not experience hunger as they were aided by a special distribution system.

The rural areas (where collectivization was implemented) were the ones first hit by starvation. At first, the urban workers received enough supplies through a rationing scheme (thus, could somehow aid their relatives who were starving in the rural areas) but the supplies were slowly tapered. In the spring of 1933, starvation eventually hit urban residents. At that time, an agitprop movie was shown to starving workers that portrayed all the peasants as insurgents who were hoarding potatoes and grains, while the workers labor hard to build socialism's "bright future".

In January 1933, the first documented evidence of death due to mass malnutrition surfaced from urban zones of Uman City. In the middle of January 1933, mass food "difficulties" were reported in metropolitan areas which received an undersupply of goods through rationing system. There were also reported deaths among starved individuals who were removed from the ration. They were removed in compliance to the Committee of the Communist Party of Ukraine Decree of December 1932. On the start of February 1933, reports by Ukrainian GPU and local authorities reported that Dnipropetrovsk Oblast was the most devastated, and that epidemic of malaria and typhus has also stricken the place. Odessa came next followed by Kiev oblast. By the middle of March, a large portion of the information about starvation came from Kiev Oblast.

By middle of April, Kharkiv Oblast topped the list of most affected areas. It was followed by Kiev, Odessa, Dnipropetrovsk, Donetsk and Vinnytsya oblasts, and lastly, Moldavian SSR. Starting mid-May to the start of June, news about mass famine deaths emerged from Kiev and Kharviv. The Central Committee passed a decree in February 1933 stating that no starvation cases should remain untreated. In compliance to the decree, local authorities were ordered to pass information on the number of people starving, the reasons of starvation and how many deaths resulted from it. Also included were the amount of food supplied by local providers, and how much centrally supplied food aid is needed. The GPU was able to give corresponding and food support in the Ukraine SSR.

Due to the extent of famine, evidence of prevalent cannibalism was recorded. To address the ensuing crime, the Soviet authority printed posters affirming: "To eat your own children is a barbarian act." During the famine, around 2,500 individuals were condemned due to cannibalism. Peasants looking for food who chose to flee to the metropolis, to the industrialized Donets Basin, or to the Russian lands were caught and transported back to their villages. Some residents of Kharkiv oblast, Kviv oblast and Poltava oblast had been totally abandoned by springtime. The majority of runaways perished together with those who were too weak or sick to attempt to flee.

In the fall of 1933, Russian peasants, chiefly from Orel oblast, began resettling in the deserted villages following the command of the Soviet regime. In the countryside of the Ukraine SSR, there was barely any agricultural activity. In the spring the same year, armed groups watched over the seeds for sowing assigned to the state. The abled peasants were tasked to plant but received hardly any rations in return. To those who managed to endure until the summer, the first harvest of vegetables and fruits saved them. The debilitating consequences of famine, illness, increased death rate and decreasing birth rate persisted for several years.

Denial of genocide

While catastrophic deaths continued, the Soviet authority kept its silence and no help was given to the sufferers during the Holodomor. Virtually unaware of the happenings in the eastern part of Ukraine, the Polish-governed Western Ukraine finally heard news and significant information regarding the famine. This incited massive civic rallies there and in the entire diaspora of

Ukrainians. In October 1933, Mykola Lemyk, an affiliate of the Organization of Ukrainian Nationalists, killed the Soviet diplomat Aleksei Mailov to draw public attention to the famine. Thereafter, Europe and North America dispatched relief operations and memoranda were sent to the League of Nations. The problem was also heard in the British parliament and Viennese Cardinal Theodor Innitzera led an international relief action. The Soviet government, however, did not receive all of this external assistance as it presses the idea that the famine was only a defamatory fabrication of the opponents of Soviet Union. To defend its side, the Soviet government invited Eduoard Herriot, the prime minister of France, to tour around Soviet Ukraine's Potemkin village. As he went back to France, Herriot stated that no proof of starvation existed and even said that the country was 'like a garden in full bloom.'

Despite foreign publications revealing Ukraine's condition, little public response was elicited from other nations. The propaganda generated a picture of a peaceful life in the USSR. In Moscow, Ukrainians who fled to the city to beg for food managed to relay to Western journalists about the true conditions in their homeland. Yet, a British journalist named Malcolm Muggeridge was ignored after releasing his reports about the holodomor. When a Welsh correspondent named Gareth Jones arrived at Ukraine and saw the ravaged nation, his eyewitness story shocked the nations. However, just as how the Kremlin strictly looks over the broadcasting in Moscow in the present times, British and American correspondents were pressured to release commentaries pointing out that Jones fabricated stories. Prominent intellectuals, most notably, George Bernard Shaw affirmed the unspoiled conditions of the Soviet Union. A. As stated by Walter Duranty in the New York Times "There is no actual starvation or deaths from starvation but there is widespread mortality from diseases due to malnutrition." In later years, research suggested that Jones was murdered by the chief security agency of the Soviet Union, the KGB.

Death toll

The Holodomor resulted to a colossal mortality rate that in some areas, 20 to 25 percent of the population were wiped out. The official invalidity and non-release of the 1937 Soviet census may suggest disastrous population drop as a result of the famine. The estimation of death toll by early scholars and government officials varies greatly. It is said that 1.8 to 12 million ethnic Ukrainians perished from the starvation. Following the Kyiv Appellation Court's decision, the demographic losses as result of famine is said to reach 10 million, with 3.9 million deaths due to starvation, and a 6.1 million birth deficit. The maximum of ten million deaths has been cited by President Viktor Yushchenko while for several years

7 million deaths was the figure usually cited. Some 1950-1960 Western scholars (M. Prykhodko, D. Solovei, W. H. Chamberlin, and V. I. Hryshko) approximated the count as 3 million to 4 million, while C. A. Manning suggested a loss of 2 million to 3 million. Recent researchers narrowed the figures between 2.4 and 7.5 million.

Due to lack of information available to the public, the exact number of deaths is difficult to determine. However, the figure escalates considerably when deaths within thickly Ukrainian-populated Kuban are included. Because of such, the devastation caused by the Holodomor has been compared to the Holocaust.

Holodomor and the present times

The present conflict of Russia and Ukraine is said to have its deepest roots in the Ukrainian famine-genocide that happened a century ago. The dramatic dwindling of nationalism in the East Ukraine (who were once as Ukrainian-speaking and patriotic as Western Ukraine today) is said to be the consequence of holodomor. Although scholarly evidence and public protests points to the famine as genocide, pro-Russian and former Ukrainian President Viktor Yanukovych insisted that the famine was not an act of intended killings. The year 2013 coincidentally marked the 80th anniversary of the famine. This sparked the anti-government protesters in Ukraine's capital, Kiev, to topple and behead the statue of Soviet state founder Vladimir Ilyich Lenin in December 18, 2013. More than relaying a message to present Russian President Putin, it served as a deed of vengeance for Soviet killings. Putin's attempt to control the media when he shot down Russia's premier broadcasting company, RIA Novosti, is said to have reminded the Ukrainian people of the media blackout during the *Holodomor*.

As said by Timothy Snyder, Yale history professor and author of *Bloodlands: Europe Between Hitler and Stalin,* Ukraine's suffering was far greater than Russia under Stalin. For Ukraine to join the European Union suggests more than economic agility and opportunities; it implies breaking political ties with Putin, who is said to be the present-day Stalin.

Chapter 7 - The Second World War

On August 23, 1939, the secret Molotov-Ribbentrop Pact was signed, which gave USSR and Nazi Germany their own shares of the Eastern Europe. On 1 September, Poland was occupied by Germany and thus beginning World War II. Soon after, Germany invaded the Podlachia, the Kholm and Lemko region, and Galicia. Assuming that Germany was the key to their independence from Polish occupation, the Western Ukrainians forged allegiance with the Germans. Until the end of September 1939, 600 men from both Carpathian Sich and the Organization of Ukrainian Nationalists acted as the intercessors of the entire populace and the advancing Nazi military.

Germany formed what is known as the Generalgouvernement (GG) of Poland in the lands it invaded. GG served as a refuge for around 20,000 Ukrainians who fled Western Ukraine east Buh and Sian River as it was being invaded by the Soviet Army; Ukrainians from Bukovyna joined the war refugees in 1940. There, frontrunners of the Organization of Ukrainian Nationalists formed a public umbrella group from November 1939 to April 1940. In June 1940, the Germans gave authorization to the Ukrainian Central Committee (UTsK), with Volodymyr Kubijovyča as its leader.

Due to Generalgouvernement's condition, most of the frontrunners of the Western Ukrainian parties who fled there were not able to openly participate in political undertakings. The only group initially allowed by the Germans was the Organization of

Ukrainian Nationalists (OUN) led by Roman Sushko, who were leading anti-Polish movements even before the war. In February 1940, the OUN was divided into two parties. One party was headed by Andrii Melnyk (since August 1939), which supported the schemes of the exile leadership, and the other faction headed by Stepan Banderal, which was committed to the standpoints of those who lead revolutions against the Polish rule in Western Ukraine. In June 1941, the two factions attempted at unifying the active political groups of Ukrainians before the German-Soviet War broke out. They aimed at working hand in hand with these groups so they could forge a battle against the Soviet, and subsequently launch an independent Ukraine.

In September 17-23 1939, Volhynia and Galica was invaded by the Soviets. On October 22, Ukrainians had to select the members of the People's Assembly of Western Ukraine following the procedures of Soviet elections. The assembly lobbied a request for the reunion of Western Ukraine and the Ukrainian SSR. In a fury response, a policy that commands extensive Sovietization was proclaimed. Mass detention of Ukrainian frontrunners who weren't able to escape and the takeover of all national institutes and assemblies of Ukraine accompany it. Since the domination of the Soviet authorities, the Polish withdrew control over national and administrative institutes, while the Ukrainians flocked to the municipalities and started

Ukrainianizing them. Numerous Jews and Polish colonists were also exiled to the east by the Soviet authorities. These reforms, nevertheless, were not able to match the overall Soviet persecution of Ukrainians and the fear that resulted.

On 28 June 1940, the USSR invaded the northern Bessarabia and Bukovyna, which were occupied by the Rumanians. On August 2, both of them were formally assimilated into the Soviet Union. Reforms in these territories are comparable to what occurred in Western Ukraine, and the official language of Rumanian was substituted by the Ukrainian language.

On June 22 1941, Germany occupied the Soviet Union, revealing the flaws of the Soviet regime and the lack of allegiance between the oppressed territories and the Soviet, especially Ukraine. Numerous members of the Soviet army fled, while many more succumbed to the Germans all together. This resulted to the quick invasion of the Germans towards the east, and by the end of 1941 they successfully occupied virtually all of Ukrainian grounds. As they were caught unprepared, the Soviet army disbanded in an unsystematic way and sought refuge in the Ural Mountains west of Ukraine.

In Lutsk, Lviv, Rivne, Zolochiv and elsewhere, around 15,000 political hostages were executed by the Communist secret police known as the NKVD. The Soviets took advantage of the termination of German activity along the Dnieper River, demolishing government and industrial structures, railways and foodstuff. They blew up the Hydroelectric station of Dnieper, a huge portion of Kharviv, central Kviv (not sparing the

Khreshchatyk boulevard) and Berdychiv; they also submerged the Donbaswere mines. As a consequence of this earth-scorching scheme, Ukraine largely suffered.

At the beginning of the warfare, Ukrainian SSR's government and many establishments of the Academy of Sciences of the Ukrainian SSR were relocated to Ufa. In the following years, several reforms were made to encourage Ukrainian nationalism, including the release of more neutral accounts of the history of Ukraine and more publications using the Ukrainian language. These were the Germans' attempt to gain the support of the masses.

In August 1941, Galicia was incorporated to the Generalgouvernement and became one of its districts; many Ukrainian territories were incorporated into the Reichskommissariat Ukraine. Meanwhile, the north of Bukovyna was reinvaded by the Rumanians, part of Bessarabia, as well as Transnistria. Transcarpathia, on the other hand, remained dominated by Hungarian authorities.

Before the invasion, the Legion of Ukrainian Nationalists (lead by Nachtigall and Roland) were formed by the Organization of Ukrainian Nationalists or OUN (Bandera faction) to counter the Bolsheviks. During the occupation, the two factions of the OUN dispatched OUN expeditionary assemblies including exiles and Western Ukrainians into eastern and central Ukraine. They were tasked to reconstruct the cultural and political life Ukrainian political life in those lands.

On 30 June 1941, the Proclamation of Ukrainian statehood of 1941 was announced by the OUN (Bandera faction) in Lviv. It resulted to the establishment of the Ukrainian State Administration led by Yaroslav Stetsko. In early July 1941, however, the members of the administration were captured by the Germans—they then continued to subdue the Bandera faction and relocated its members to concentration camps. However, as opposed to such suppressions, a number of German dominions (most remarkably the Ostministerium of Rosenberg and the Abwehr) offered protection to the Banderites, including some of its militants.

In July 1941, a second Ukrainian national council (after the Central Rada) known as the Ukrainian National Council in Lviv, 1941 had been formed through the direction of Metropolitan Andrei Sheptytsky. It was led by Kost Levytsky and embodied the people of Ukraine before the Germans. The council intensely objected Galicia's integration into the GG up until the German authorities barred it in March 1942. In September 1941, the Germans permitted Ukrainian Regional Committee under the leadership of Kost K. Pankivsky to act as an umbrella organization. In March 1942, however, its responsibilities were handed over to the Cracow-based Ukrainian Central Committee. Pankivsky became the Committee leader Volodymyr Kubijovyč's closest associate at that time.

On September 19, Kyviv was invaded by the Germans and in the following month, O. Olzhych and other associates from the OUN (Melnyk faction) created a Ukrainian National Council in Kyiv. Mykola Velychkivsky then became the leader of the Ukrainian civic-political center. In December 1941, the German authority curbed the activities of the council and detained its chief patriots (including M. Teliha, O. Teliha, I. Irliavsky, I. Rohach and O. Chemerynsky). They were then killed two months after, which obligated the Melnyk faction to become a clandestine group.

Most territories of Ukraine (the Reichskommissariat Ukraine) suffered under the cruel leader Erick Kock. Rivne-based Kock mandated frightful policies and did intense abuse to the population, which was considered inhumane. Until 1943, the Germans did not abolish the collective farm system implemented by Stalin during the holodomor. Private trading (excluding cooperatives and indigenous markets) was prohibited and a substantial amount of raw materials and foodstuff were seized from the Ukrainians. Soon after, cultural groups and institutes were prohibited while the only ones permitted to operate were four-year elementary schools. The press (around 115 periodicals) was run and sternly regulated by the Germans. Despite of the support of some German groups on the revival and inauguration of the Ukrainian Autocephalous Orthodox church, the Reichskommissariat administration did not allow its existence as it was technically a subordinate of the Moscow patriarch.

Throughout the extent of the German invasion, 6.8 million people of Ukraine were executed, of which around 1.4 million were Soviet military forerunners (who lost life during battle or famished in concentration camps) and an equal number were Jews. Starting February 1942, greater than 2 million Ukrainians were resettled to Germany as slave workers. The annihilation and dread experienced by the Ukrainians under the Nazi incited widespread aggression and ensue military and political upheavals. Patriotic supporters based in Volhynia structured what is known as Polisian Sich and changed the name of Ukrainian Insurgent Army (UPA). Through the leadership of T. Borovets (Bulba), they fought against the receding Soviet Army following the invasion. From the spring of 1942 until 1945, the group waged wars against both the Soviet patriots and Germans that occupied Ukraine.

When the German troops were vanquished at Stalingard in the beginning of the year 1943, there had been a marked increase in armed confrontations within Ukraine. In the spring of the same year, thousands of Ukrainian ancillary policemen left the German and joined the OUN (Bandera faction). Because of this, the UON (Bandera faction) played a remarkable role as a partisan force. However, the Banderites gained force and became abled enough to defuse the partisan groups who were supporting the OUN (Melnyk faction) and Taras Borovets. The Banderites, with its own partisan groups, then assumed the title of the Ukrainian Insurgent Army (UPA) and operated under the leadership of Roman Shukhevych. The UPA successfully ousted the Germans in the Volhynian countryside in May 1943. Thereafter, the UPA (under SydirKovpak) annexed into Galicia to overthrow the offensive Soviet-partisan and to maintain war efforts against the Germans and the mountain soldiers of Polish Home Army. In July 1944, the leaders of UPA launched the Ukrainian

Supreme Liberation Council and made it political leader of the nationwide Ukrainian underground movement. The council persisted on its battle with Soviet rule and domination until the 1950s.IIt also circulated an autonomous program implemented by the OUN (Bandera faction) in 1943.

By mid-1943, the offensive Soviet army pressured the Germans to start withdrawing from Ukraine. In Eastern Ukraine, the Nazis created massive devastation in Poltava Dnipropetrovsk, Kyiv, Kremenchuk, and several other cities. By the spring of 1944, the army reached Western Ukraine and afterward set foot on the Division Galizien—a Ukrainian formation within the German army created in 1943. The Division Galizien was considered by its organizers as the core of independent Ukraine`s future army. However, it was extensively devastated at the Battle of Brody. By October month-end of 1943, the entire Ukrainian territory once again fell under the Soviet rule.

In autumn of 1944, just as when almost the entire Ukraine was reinvaded by the Soviet Union, the Germans started to change their treatment of the Ukrainian population. They freed political frontrunners imprisoned in concentration camps, such as Y. Stetsko S. Bandera, A. Melnyk and T. Borovets. In March 1945, the Germans acknowledged the Ukrainian National Committee (UNK) led by Volodymyr Kubijovyč, Gen Pavlo Shandruk, and Oleksander Semenenko. These leaders became the representative of the people of Ukraine in the Third Reich. The Committee, however, cannot perform many functions aside from saving the fragments of Division Galizien and assimilating them into other Ukrainian formations within the German army (such as the Ukrainian Liberation Army). Their purpose was supposedly to build a Ukrainian National Army out of these assimilations, but they surrendered to the British after the defeat of Germany.

Chapter 8 - Post-Soviet Russia and Ukraine Disputes

The disintegration of the Soviet Union in 1991 caused several disputes among the successor states. Specifically, the Russian-Ukrainian ties were seriously constrained. The scope of their dispute is rather wide--concerning ethnic, political, military, economic, and territorial issues. For Russia, it has been particularly difficult to accept Ukraine's separation, which it considered as its "little brother". Meanwhile, the Ukrainians who has just gained their official political independence wanted to establish their own identity as a separate East Slavic nation.

Both Russians and Ukrainians are searching for their individual identities as much as both Moscow and Kiev are aiming as much economic, military and political gains from USSR's downfall. For this reason, long-term disputes arose and are still existent even two decades later.

1990s

After the dissolution of the Soviet Union, a number of severe disputes ensued between Russia and Ukraine. The first dispute concerned Crimea, which had been part of the Ukrainian SSR since 1954 through an executive order of the Russian Federation's Presidium of the Supreme Council. The conflict, however, was resolved through a treaty that permitted Crimea to stay under the jurisdiction of Ukraine, so long as it retains its status as an autonomous republic. Another clash of the 90s occurred with Sevastopol City, which has the Black Sea Fleet base. Sevastopol city, unlike the Crimean peninsula, possesses a distinct standing under the USSR. During the dissolution of the Soviet Union During the dissolution of the Soviet Union, Sevastopol and all of Ukraine took part in the nationwide poll for Ukraine's independence where around 60 percent of the populace voted for Ukraine to rule over Sevastopol. In 1993, the Supreme Soviet of Russia aimed at reclaiming its power over the city. The vote, however, was not acknowledged by Russian President Boris Yeltsin because he and the Parliament were at a gridlock at that time. Following many years of stern discussions, the conflict was settled in 1997 by dividing the Black Sea Fleet and chartering several Sevastopol naval bases to the Russians until 2017.

The third major conflict between the two nations concerned energy supply, since a number of gas and oil pipelines of Western Europe and the Soviet nations pass through Ukrainian grounds. Afterwards, as new agreements were made, Ukraine's huge debt to Russia had been remunerated through the surrender of nuclear resources and Soviet artillery (e.g. the Tu-160 bombers) to Russia. Also during this decade, both Ukraine and Russia, together with former Soviet members constituted the Commonwealth of Independent States which gave way to huge industrial partnership among them.

From 1997 until 2000, Russia's share in the exports of Ukraine dropped, while the import shares remained stable. In general, the Russian SFSR held around 1/3 to 1/2 of Ukraine's trades. Ukraine had been strongly dependent on Russia in terms of energy supply that around 80 percent of oil and 70-75 percent of gas expended yearly are supplied by Russia. Substantial dependence was also seen in terms of export as Ukraine remained Russia's chief supplier of pipes and steel plate, ferrous metals, mechanical tools, electric machinery, food, and chemical industry products. The Russian market has been highly valued by Ukraine since greater than nine-tenth of its goods were traditionally linked to Russian buyers. In 1997, however, there had been a plunge of 97 to 99 percent in the manufacture of digitally-controlled industrial machineries, TV sets, excavators, tape recorders, trucks and cars. Meanwhile, Russia emerged as one of the biggest investors in the economy of Ukraine, next to the US, Netherlands, and Germany despite of its economic sluggishness since the dissolution of the Soviet Union. By 1998, Russia was able to invest about $151 million out of $2 billion foreign investments directly obtained by Ukraine from all sources.

2000s

Despite of several disputes before the 2004 presidential elections in Ukraine, the nation's relationship with Russia improved under Leonid Kuchma's leadership in the latter years. Such conflicts included the speculations that the Ukrainian military accidentally shot down a commercial Russian airbus and the dispute over Tuzla Island. In the year 2002, the erection of the Rivne and Khmelnitsky nuclear plants was made possible by the funding offered by the Russian government. However, several conflicts emerged following the Orange Revolution (series of protests against 2014 presidential election fraud) such as a natural gas dispute and the impending membership of Ukraine to North Atlantic Treaty Organization (NATO).

Because of historical events, different regions of Ukraine have different views on the relationship of Ukraine and Russia. Majority of southern and eastern Ukrainians acclaim Russia's exploits since they have strong historical links with the country. On the other hand, central and western regions of Ukraine (which are Polish-ruled and were never under the Russian empire) express an unwelcoming attitude.

Meanwhile in Russia, the opinion about Ukraine is generally singular but its current efforts to join NATO and the European Union is considered anti-Russian pro-Western expression, thus an act of hostility. This caused the deterioration of Ukraine's view of Russia despite the effort of Ukraine President Yushchenko to defend the country's motives of joining the NATO. The conflict was further aggravated by Ukrainian's public discourse whether to officialise the Russian language as the country's second language. In the peak of the gas conflict of 2009, almost all the media coverage in Russian talk of Ukraine as hostile and acquisitive nation that prefers to forge alliance with the enemies of Russia and exploit the low-cost Russian gas. The conflict was worsened further because of provocative statements of both Ukrainian and Russian political leaders. In addition, the Black Sea Fleet of Russian in Sevastopol continues to be a subject for dispute and tension.

Second Term of Tymoshenko

In February 2008, the 1997 intergovernmental agreement on SPRN between Russia and Ukraine was dissolved after the unilateral withdrawal of Russia. During the war between Russia and Georgia war, Ukraine offered support and sold weapons to Georgia, which further soured its relations with Russia. Through investigations carried out by Russia, Ukraine's army was accused of alliance with Gregorian forces together with 200 Ukrainian UNA-UNSO members. Further arguments about Ukraine's stand on the Georgian and Russian conflict led to the total breakdown of Our Ukraine-Peoples Self Defence + Bloc Yulia Tymoshenko coalition in September 2008. Three months after, however, the coalition merged with a different partner, the Lytvyn Bloc.

During the war in South Ossetia in 2008, Ukraine had set new guidelines for Russia stating that the Russian Black Sea Fleet should ask for authorization first before it can cross the borders of Ukraine. Russia has strongly rebuffed such rules.

On October 2008 Ukraine was indicted by Putin for providing weaponries to Georgia during the Ossetia War. The Russian Prime Minister also claimed that Moscow gathered proof about the presence of Ukrainian military specialists in the war zone. Ukraine however denied such accusations. Defense Minister Yuriy Yekhanurov claimed that no military expert from Ukraine sided with Georgia; meanwhile, Ukrspetsexport, the leading company of Ukrainian's weaponry export declared that it did not sell any weapons during the war. These statements were affirmed by Ukrainian General Prosecutor on September 25, 2009, pressing that Armed Forces of Ukraine is not involved in the 2008 South Ossetia War, no military paraphernalia of the Ukrainian

Armed Forces were used at the war zone, and no aid was provided by Ukraine to Georgia. It is further stated that during 2006-2008, all interstate transfer of army equipment between Georgia and Ukraine was done in compliance with previous agreements, the Ukrainian laws and with international settlements.

In January 2009, a conflict on natural gas price emerged resulting to the shutdown of Russian oil which passes through Ukraine. The state relations further worsened when Putin stated that the political leaders of Ukraine is displaying incapacity to address trade and industry problems and certain circumstances points out to its highly criminalized state authorities. After the dispute (February 2009), Russian President Medvedev stated that Ukraine needed to pay damages to the European countries because of losses incurred during the gas crisis. However, both President Yushchenko and the Ukrainian Foreign Ministry believed that Medvedev's statement was emotional, and is unfavorable and antagonistic towards the European Union member-states as well as towards Ukraine. While the conflict was heated up, the media coverage all throughout Russia almost always showed Ukraine being antagonistic and acquisitive that planned to collaborate with the enemies of Russia and abuse the low-cost Russian natural gas.

On March 23, 2009, a "master plan" to remodel the Ukrainian natural gas groundwork was signed between Ukraine and the European Union. During the conference where such plan was declared, Russian Energy Minister Shmatko stated that the treaty might affect Moscow's welfare as it seemed to pull Ukraine closer to the European Union in legal terms. In addition, Prime Minister Putin said that it is frivolous to deliberate on such matters without the presence of the basic gas supplier, which is Russia.

In January 2009, a US diplomatic cable leak showed former Ambassador of Ukraine to Russia Kostyantyn Hryshchenko saying that the Russian authority sought to witness Ukraine being completely submissive to Kremlin. It is also said that Vladimir Putin has hatred for former President Yushchenko. He also had little personal respect for Viktor Yanukovych but considered former Prime Minister Tymoshenko as somehow he can deal with, though he cannot trust.

On 11 August 2009, Russian President Medvedev created a video blog wherein he criticized Viktor Yushchenko, for being responsible in their deteriorating state relations and for present Ukrainian authorities' anti-Russian attitudes. Consequent to this supposed sentiment, Medvedev declared that no Russian ambassador will be placed in Ukraine unless there is a progress of their relationship. Ukrainian President Viktor Yushchenko then responded to this letter by Medvedev saying that he is not pleased with the current circumstances of the two states and pondered why Medvedev entirely disregards Russia's responsibly for problems in their relations. According to analysts, the statement of Medvedev was deliberately planned to coincide with and to influence the Ukrainian presidential election campaign of 2010. As a response to the video blog, the U.S. Department of said that Russia's comments were unnecessary and that Ukraine is entitled to make its own decisions;

therefore, it can join NATO if it wants. (Ever since Ukraine proposed to join NATO in the January 2008 NATO Membership Action Plan, the U.S. pledged support to the country in spite of Russia's objections).

In October 2009, Russian Foreign Minister Sergei Lavrov said that Russia aims to witness economic boost in Russian and Ukrainian lands and that their countries' relationship will greatly advance if they would establish business partnership, particularly in small and medium-sized ventures. During the same conference in Kharkiv, the Russian foreign minister said that his country does not want to a meeting between the Russian and Ukrainian presidents, but their communication will always be kept through the two countries' foreign ministries.

In December 2009, Ukrainian Foreign Minister Petro Poroshenko and Russian Foreign Minister Lavrov decided to slowly remove the prohibition on certain individuals from entering each other's countries.

2010s

Viktor Yanukovych Presidency

According to Taras Kuzio, the neo-Soviet president Viktor Yanukovych is the top Ukrainian president who highly reveres Russia. In the letter written by Yanukovych to then-President Yushnenko in August 2009, he stated that since he was elected to the office he fulfilled all of Russian President Medvedev's demands. In April 2010, a highly provocative lease agreement was signed by Ukrainian President Yanukovych and Russian President Medvedev. It stated that the Russian Naval Forces base in Sevastopol will have discount in the delivery of natural gas for the next 25 years. This accounts for $100 per 1,000 cubic meters. It sparked discussions within and outside Ukraine.

In May 2010, President Dmitry Medvedev visited Kviv to sign an agreement. He stated that his administration will collaborate in addressing inter-regional and international problems. The same issue was also discussed by First Deputy prime-minister Andriy Kliuyev at the Verkhovna Rada. Several media agencies said that the primary goal of Medvedev's visit was to settle natural gas problems between Russia and Ukraine after Viktor Yanukovych approved on the fractional union of the two state gas companies Naftogaz and Gazprom. Aside from this union there had also been discussions in the union of the nuclear energy sector. In April 2010, both the Russian and Ukranian presidents said that they have seen a huge advancement in the relations of their countries since the presidency of Viktor Yanukovych.

In May 2013, Sergei Razumovsky, the once anonymous veteran of an unfamiliar intelligence facility, who came out to be the head of the All-Ukrainian Association of Homeless Officers, proposed the establishment of a Ukrainian-Russian international volunteer taskforce. This is to back up the Syrian Bashar al-Assad government who were fight against militants. One of the reasons of Rozumovsky in establishing such taskforce was the fact that Ukraine does not provide backing for its officer corps. Since Rozumovsky has shown intent in applying for Syrian citizenship, several sources assert that he is a Russian provocateur.

In July 2013, the patrol vessel of Russian coast guard rammed into a Ukrainian fishing boat near the Russian coast of Azov Sea, which is both Russia's and Ukraine's internal waters (no border demarcation). Four Ukrainian fishermen were killed in the incident while one was held captive by Russian authorities on the charges of poaching. The surviving fisherman stated that the Russians hit their boat and fired at them as well. However, the Russian police force asserted that it was the poaching Ukrainians who attempted to run into the patrol boat. Ukraine's Minister of Justice acclaimed that Russia by any means does not have authority to prosecute the arrested Ukrainian citizen. The family of the survived fisherman stated that they received little help from the Ukrainian Consul in Russia regarding the incident. The fishermen should have been discharged from Russian custody before August 12, 2013, but Russia's Prosecutor Office opted to retain the Ukrainian within Russia.

On August 14, 2013, there had been a debarment of Ukrainian goods entering Russia as per the command of Russian Custom Service. Several political analysts saw this as the beginning of a trade war against Ukraine to prevent Ukraine from signing a trade agreement with the European Union.

On August 28, 2013, another border trespassing incident happened between Luhansk and Belgorod oblasts. A seemingly intoxicated Russian tractor driver and his two companions attempted to cross the Ukrainian border. Contrary to the Azov incident one month earlier, the State Border Service of Ukraine abdicated the Russian citizens immediately to the Russians. Meanwhile, the tractor was taken away from the three trespassers and surrendered to the Ministry Revenue and Collections.

In December 2013, President Putin approved to loan 15 billion dollars to Ukraine as economic aid and a discount of 33% on natural gas prices. Despite of intense and constant protests by Ukrainians who want to forge closer relations with the European Union, the agreement was signed. Critics pointed out that in the months before the December 17 2013 deal, Russia attempted to prevent Ukraine from signing the association agreement with the European Union by making a change in its customs regulations on imports from Ukraine.

Chapter 9 - The 2014 Ukrainian Crisis

This year, the world cautiously watched the growing volatility of Ukraine's political scene. Within Ukraine, a political schism has been formed in which the citizens of the eastern regions are against reform. As they emerged to be sympathizers of Federal Russia, Ukraine's internal conflict seemed to careen towards a war with its neighbor superpower, Russia. Acute upheavals broke across Ukraine; fights ensued between Ukrainian and Russian military troops sided by pro-Russian Ukrainian rebels. This instantly concerned international leaders as the war has great possibility of reaching a worldwide scale. They began to urge the two nations to come up with a diplomatic solution. The United States and most members of the European Union have declared economic sanctions against Russia and proposed to eliminate it from G8 if it insists on sending military troops to Ukraine.

The present conflict is rooted in Ukrainian President Viktor Yanukovych's rejection of an economic agreement with the European Union (EU) last November 2013 and instead chose to preserve closer relations with Russia. The motive of such trade agreement is rather straightforward: the EU aims to encourage more Eastern European economies to join their trade agreements, while Ukraine wants closer relations with Western counties' more advance and lucrative economies. However, when the EU's association agreement was being forged in November 2013, then Ukrainian President Viktor

Yanukovych suddenly expressed uncertainties at the last phase of signing. Ukrainians saw their president's equivocation as an apparent sign that he was put under great pressure by Russian President Vladimir Putin who wants him to abandon EU's proposal. After a few days, President Yanukovych flatly rejected the association agreement and instead accepted a new deal from Russia in a form of $15 billion financial support, together with other trade and industry aids.

President Yanukovych's submission to the Russian force instantly provoked anger among many Ukrainians. For many years, the citizens have been fighting for industrial reforms that would notch up Ukraine's economy in line with the more prosperous Western economies. Their president's rejection of the EU proposal is not merely a disregard of the desires of most Ukrainians but indicated the government's reinforced alliance with Russia. Such implications triggered a lethal upheaval among the Ukrainian citizen condemning their government for fraud and questioning the sincerity of their president's nationalism.

A few hours after Yanukovych's rejection of the EU proposal, thousands of demonstrators flocked the streets of Ukraine's capital, Kiev to voice out their yearning for economic change and their intense disapproval to the decision of their president. They demanded him to step down from his office immediately. As a reaction to the commotion, the Ukrainian government immediately deployed riot police and military forces to the protest zones all throughout the country. Tensions between the citizens and the armed men spiralled quickly and videos were even uploaded on YouTube showing the demonstrators tossing Molotov cocktails at the police while the armed guards torment the opposition.

The upheavals in Ukraine continued and escalated slowly the following months. Meanwhile, the European Union and the United States proposed new settlements for Ukraine, offering the Ukrainian authority chances to work around and honor the demands of its antagonized people.

In mid-February, however, the number of casualties in Kiev abruptly climbed to the hundreds. Chances to resolve the conflict between President Yanukovych and the opposition leaders became slimmer. On February 21, the opposition forces overtook Ukraine's capital Kiev, including Yanukovych's residence. Fearing for his life, the Ukrainian president escaped to Russia quickly while being condemned for the murder of protesters.

The overthrow of the Ukrainian president has awakened Russia to the fact its administrative influence over Ukraine was deteriorating. The Russian authority, nevertheless, pointed out that the antagonism back in Ukraine is not a legitimate threat to Yanukovych's presidential power. Russia expressed great interest in supporting Yanukovych to remain in position. A statement of the Kremlin deemed Yanukovych the rightful leader of Ukraine and that a Russian occupation is not a violation of international law since it has consent from the president. Russia also aimed at inhibiting any kind of autonomous political transformation that could draw Ukraine closer to Europe and farther away from Russia.

Following the protesters' total control over Kiev and the Ukrainian president's escape to Russia for protection, unidentified armed men started to roam around the Ukrainian-Russian border. On 27 February, the soldiers then started to quickly intrude the Ukrainian province of Crimea. The Crimean peninsula, roughly the size of Massachusetts, is an autonomous republic within Ukraine consisting of a huge Russophone population (59% are ethnic Russians) who generally identify themselves more closely with Russia than Ukraine. In addition, Crimea is the site of a number of robust Russian naval bases.

The armed men overtook several principal establishments in the province, including the two airports and the parliament building. They ruined virtually all internet and phone connection between Crimea and the rest of Ukraine. While under siege, the autonomous republic's government laid off the Supreme Council of Crimea and supplanted the chairman of the Council of Ministers of Crimea Anatolii Mohyliov with pro-Moscow leader Sergey Aksyonov.

On 1 March, after a plea for assistance from Sergey Aksyonov and after getting the approval of the Parliament, Russian President Putin called for a military movement consisting of more than 100,000 troops. On the same day, the Ukraine's acting president Oleksandr Turchynov declared the appointment of the Crimean Prime Minister as unconstitutional. He considered the actions of the Russian government as a deliberate hostility towards the autonomy of Ukraine.

By March 2, Russians had assumed full military control of the Crimean peninsula and continued to preserve the seizure of Ukraine's military installations in the region. Putin argued that the Russian citizens and military based in Crimea needed his protection from the political instability of Ukraine; however, Ukrainian officials dispute such claims and reproached Russia for overriding the Ukraine's internal affairs. This careful expression of Russian force seemed to convey a message that Russia was ready to wage a war against Ukraine. On the same day, the Parliament has also approved President Putin's request to drive more military troops into Ukraine. This sent waves of alarm all around the globe since the potential Russian annexation of Crimea had drawn the Russian and Ukrainian forces closer towards brutal conflict.

The U.S., together with other G7 leaders (Canada, Germany, France, Japan, Italy, and the United Kingdom), strongly disapproved the aggression of Russia. In a statement, U.S. President Obama considered Russia's behaviour a "clear violation of Ukraine's sovereignty and territorial integrity which is a breach of international law, including Russia's obligations under the UN Charter, and of its 1997 military basing agreement with Ukraine" that "would negatively impact Russia's standing in the international community." He has also firmly stressed his stand that a new government should be launched by Ukraine and that it must get ready for election by spring. Meanwhile, he reprimanded Russia to withdraw its force from Ukraine. EU leaders have also deliberated on several economic sanctions against Russia, asset freezes, and an arms embargo. On March 5, U.S. Secretary of State John

Kerry held a meeting with British, German and French foreign ministers in an attempt to dissolve the crisis.

On March 6, the Parliament of Crimea created an appeal to be integrated to the Russian Federation. A referendum was planned on March 16 where Crimean citizens could vote on the appeal. However, a Ukrainian government minister stated that it is unconstitutional for Crimea to be integrated to Russia. Western diplomats then tried to hold dialogues to stop Russia from initiating a complete invasion of Ukraine.

On 11 March, the Parliament of Crimea voted and ratified a declaration of independence of the city of Sevastopol and the Autonomous Republic of Crimea from Ukraine. Seventy eight out of 100 voted in favor of the establishment of the Republic of Crimea. On March 16, the planned referendum was held and the Republic of Crimea acknowledged its independence from Ukraine. The following day, it began pursuing for United Nations' recognition, and appealed to unite with the Russian Federation. On the same day, the Russian Federation accepted Crimea as a sovereign state.

On March 27, the U.N. General Assembly decreed a non-binding Resolution 68/262 stating that referendum held in Crimea was unconstitutional and the integration of Crimea into Federal Russia is invalid. On the same day, the International Monetary Fund (IMF) declared a loan agreement for Ukraine worth $14-18 billion to support reforms and help stabilize the economy of Ukraine. The U.S. Senate also declared $1 billion worth of loan guarantees to Ukraine, together with sanctions against Russia.

On March 28, the United Nations proclaimed the March 16 Crimean referendum as unconstitutional as it violated the Ukrainian law. The United Nations also stated it will not allow Russia to claim Crimea. Meanwhile, Russia disapproved the resolution of the United Nations, claiming that it only obscures efforts to solve the conflict.

On March 28, President Obama talked with President Putin by phone for about 90 minutes. As said by the White House; the Russian president wanted to discuss about an American proposal "for a diplomatic resolution to the crisis," trying to stop the emerging tensions between Russia, Ukraine and other world leaders. The two head of states decided that their individual top diplomats "would meet to discuss next steps." President Obama stated that the conflict would be solved only if Russia withdraws its military troops from Ukraine. However, according to a report made by the Kremlin about the phone talk, Russia remains steadfast to its goal to safeguard its interests in Ukraine, particularly in the province of Crimea.

In mid-April, pro-Russian militants overtook establishments in around 10 cities and towns across Ukraine's industrial centers (in the eastern provinces). In response, Ukraine's Acting President Olexander Turchynov declared the beginning of anti-militant operations in the Donetsk region of Ukraine. Meanwhile, President Obama urged Putin to force resignation among militants in Donetsk and other parts of eastern Ukraine. Nations around the globe were again distressed since the action of the

Ukrainians against the militants might spark up a full-blown Russian invasion.

On April 17, representatives from the EU, Ukraine, Russia, and the US convened in Geneva and came to settlement that no party would induct "violence, intimidation, or provocative actions" and that all "illegal armed groups will be disarmed." Additionally, all the establishments which were unlawfully seized must be surrendered to respective legal owners and all unlawfully occupied public places (including streets and squares) all throughout Ukraine's towns and cities must be cleared out immediately.

In late April, the Russian government and the US were unsuccessful in fulfilling the provisions of the April 17 agreement, which aimed to end the conflict. Ukraine declared that any trespassing of Russian military to the Ukrainian territory will be considered an invasion, and that they will counterattack with force.

On May 1, Acting President Olexander Turchynov recalled for military mobilization and gave caution that Ukraine is on "full combat alert". Pro-Russian rebels in eastern Doestsk then overtook the regional prosecutor's office. The following day, Turchynov stated that many of the rebels had been injured, arrested and killed in a government attack in the eastern Sloviansk city. Pro-Russians shot down two army helicopters, killing its Ukrainian pilot and another serviceman. Meanwhile in the Black Sea city of Odessa, armed encounters left at least 42 people dead. Most of the casualties were pro-Russian activists who were caught in a fire inside a building they had fortified themselves. On May 3, the seven international military observers held captive in Sloviansk for seven days were released by the pro-Russian gunmen.

On May 4, Pro-Russian rebels initiated a firing encounter with Odessa police headquarters, pressuring the police to let go of dozens of people held captive during the earlier commotion. Meanwhile, Interim PM Arseniy Yatsenyuk stated that the inefficiency of the police resulted to the fire that previously engulfed several people. Three days later, a Russian policy reform became apparent when President Putin appealed to suspend the referendums in eastern Ukraine in order to motivate negotiations. He also described the presidential elections in Ukraine which was scheduled in 25 May as a move going "in the right direction".

On May 19, Russian President Putin stated that he commanded the withdrawal of military troops near Ukraine's border. However, according to NATO no sign of withdrawal was seen. Three days later, rebels attacked and killed 14 soldiers on checkpoint in Volnovakha, east of Ukraine.

On May 25, Ukraine conducted the scheduled presidential election but most voting stations in the east remained non-operational. Petro Poroshenko won the elections who then promised to bring "peace to a united and free Ukraine". The following day, the Ukrainian army initiated the anti-terrorist operation to overthrow the pro-Russian rebels occupying the Donetsk airport. At least 40 rebels were killed after Ukraine's deployment of helicopters, combat jets, and airborne troops. Russian authority then told President-elect Poroshenko that it is open to talk about the conflict but pressed that military activity against the rebels should be stopped.

On May 29, the Pro-Russian separatist rebels near Sloviansk shot down a military helicopter, leaving 14 people dead. The next day, interim Defence Minister Mykhailo Koval said that the Ukrainian military will continue its attack against the separatists until peace and order are restored in the east. On June 3, NATO agreed to strengthen its defences as a response to Russian attacks in Ukraine, but it maintains to comply with a key agreement it had with Moscow.

On June 4, US President Barack Obama condemned Russia for its aggressive acts towards Ukraine while delivering a speech in Warsaw (marking the 25th years since the dissolution of communism in Poland). Meanwhile in Ukraine, the rebels overtook two military bases in the eastern part of Luhansk as aggressions carried on near the town of Sloviansk, which they had occupied earlier. In the following day, the leaders of the G7 industrial nations encouraged Russia to start dialogue with the new Ukrainian president in Kiev with aims to terminate the crisis in east Ukraine. This resulted to a call for an immediate termination of bloodshed by both Russian President Vladimir Putin and Ukrainian President-elect Petro Poroshenko.

On June 10, President Poroshenko commanded the establishment of humanitarian efforts to help civilians escape the regions in eastern Ukraine hit by the war. On June 12, Ukraine saw three Russian armored tanks entering the east, but the accusation was sharply denied by Russia. The following day, the Ukrainian military troops recovered the port city of Mariupol after intense encounter with separatist rebels. On June 14, a vicious unrest outside the Russian embassy in Ukraine resulted in the smashing of windows and overturning of cars. Meanwhile, pro-Russia separatists shot down a military plane in the east, killing 49 people.

On June 16, Russia cut off all gas supplies to Ukraine since it failed to pay its debts, said Gazprom. Meanwhile, fighting continued in eastern Ukraine killing Russian state TV journalist Igor Kornelyuk during a mortar attack near a village outside Luhansk. On June 20, President Poroshenko proclaimed a 15-point peace proposal and declared a 7-day armistice. The next day, the U.S. enforced sanctions against several pro-Russian rebels in Ukraine.

Though the rebels approved the armistice as proposed by the Ukrainian government, they said on Jun 23 that they will not remove their weapons until the government military leaves eastern Ukraine. On the following day, a Ukrainian military helicopter was shot down in the east, leaving nine people dead. According to the UN, fighting in eastern Ukraine has already killed more than 420 people since April 15.

On June 25, the Parliament of Russia dropped off a government resolution approving the use of Russian forces in Ukraine. European Union leaders applauded such decision but notified that it will give more sanctions against Russia if it would not carry out more means to curb the conflicts in Ukraine. Two days after, an association agreement was signed by Ukraine and the EU, along with Georgia and Moldova, in what President Poroshenko defined as the most significant day in Ukraine's history since its independence in 1991. At the 26 June 2014 gathering of the Parliamentary Assembly of the Council of Europe, President Poroshenko said that Ukraine's relationship with Russia would not stabilize unless Russia disengages its occupation of Crimea and hand it over to Ukraine.

Economic implications of the Ukrainian Crisis

Why is Russia very much concerned with economic agreements Ukraine makes with other countries or international organizations? One reason could be that Russia fears about an economic setback if Ukraine settled such agreements, and in particular, the association agreement with the European Union. This contract will result to an immense inflow of superior yet affordable European goods to Ukraine. A considerable proportion of these merchandises would unavoidably reach Russia and would not be subjected to tariffs since Russia and Ukraine had signed free-trade agreements. Additionally, Russia still holds onto its regional supremacy over Ukraine though the Cold War is over. An economic agreement between Ukraine and EU potentially undercuts Russia's image as a formidable world power.

The current Russian military upheavals have contributed to the substantial fall in Russian rubble and stocks. The market considered Russian hostility as an egregious choice, and the trade and industry of Russia will likely persist on plunging with further incitements. Severe economic sanctions against Russia, however, could negatively affect the economies of Italy and Germany more than Russia because oil shortage and price inflation would certainly follow. Russia is the lead supplier of oil for a huge part of Europe, and this commodity happens to pass through Ukraine. A severe clash or an escalation of the present conflict would almost undoubtedly lead to quick price inflation within the European Union. Additionally, the Russian economy seems to have less struggle working around the sanctions especially because its geographically and politically close neighbor, China, is there to possibly supply some of its commercial necessities.

Chapter 10 - Key Information about Crimea (*A Special Coverage*)

The Crimean peninsula-- the main breaking point in the current Ukrainian crisis— is a pro-Russia part of Ukraine, and is separated geographically, historically and politically from the rest of the country. On 11 March, the Parliament of Crimea voted and ratified a declaration of independence of the city of Sevastopol and the Autonomous Republic of Crimea from Ukraine. Seventy eight out of 100 voted in favor of the establishment of the Republic of Crimea. On March 16, the Republic of Crimea officially acknowledged its independence from Ukraine.

Location

The Crimean province spreads towards the Black Sea and covers all islands except for one narrow belt of land northward, which connects it to the central land. On the east of Crimea, a strip of land almost spreads out to Russia. Russia proposed to create a bridge across this strait separating it from Crimea.

The Crimean peninsula is slightly smaller than Belgium, covering 27,000 square kilometers (10,000 square miles) land area. Its capital is Simferopol and it is the only lawful autonomous region of Ukraine. Meanwhile, Sevastopol has a distinct position within Ukraine.

Crimea is renowned in Western countries as the area of the Yalta Conference held in 1945 in which U.S. President Franklin Roosevelt, USSR leader Josef

Stalin and British Prime Minister Winston Churchill co-signed the partition of Europe after the world war.

History

In the 18th century, Catherine the Great of Russia annexed Crimea into the Russian empire, together with most of ethnic Ukrainian lands. Soon afterwards, the Black Sea naval base of Russia was founded in Sevastopol.

During the Crimean War of 1853-56 between the Ottoman Empire (supported by France and Britain) and Russia, approximately 500,000 people were killed. The conflict changed Europe's political landscape and paved the way for the First World War.

In 1921, the Crimean peninsula then inhabited mostly by Muslim Tatars, was integrated to the Soviet Union. Soviet dictator Joseph Stalin deported Tatars en masse at the dawn of Second World War for their suspected alliance with the German Nazis.

Why Ukraine Owns Crimea

It was only in 1954 that Crimea was integrated to Ukraine after USSR leader Nikita Khrushchev gave it to his homeland. However, this was barely significant until the USSR was dissolved in 1991 and the peninsula was lawfully handed over to an independent Ukraine. However, about 60 percent of 2 million Crimean citizens recognize themselves as Russians. Following the breakdown of the Soviet Union in 1991, several political commotions between Kiev and Moscow ensued about Crimea's territorial status.

Population

Around 2 million people reside in Crimea and a 2001 census showed that about 58 percent were ethnic Russian, 24 percent were ethnic Ukrainian and 12 percent were Tatars (who backs up the new pro-Western government in Ukraine).

The Tatars

When the USSR fell in 1991, the once brutally evicted Tatars (under Stalin in 1944) went back to Crimea. They were the land's native hosts before Catherine the Great of Russia occupied it in 1700s. The Tatars of Crimea, who presently comprises around 12% of Crimean population, sought alliance with the anti-Yanukovych activists in Kiev.

Economy

Yalta, among other temperate areas of Crimea, is a famous destination for both Ukrainian and Russian tourists. It was where the victors of the Second World War—the Soviet, U.S. and Britain--convened in 1945 to talk about the prospective changes they will make in Europe.

Crimea contributes three percent of the gross domestic product (GDP) of Ukraine, wherein 60% of its yield is composed of services. The land is heavily planted, with sunflowers, corn and wheat as its primary crops. Additional supply of water is brought in by a canal extending form Ukraine's Dnieper River. It also has several chemical processing plants and an iron ore quarry could be found in Kerch. Crimea also houses two of Ukraine's grain terminals.

The black sea fleet

The city of Sevastopol, located on the southern shore of Crimea, houses the Russian Black Sea Fleet and its thousands of marine workforces. Half of Russia's Soviet fleet is stationed here. Russia's Black Sea base in Sevastopol allows Moscow to have access to the Mediterranean. Meanwhile, the Ukraine's fleet, shaped out similar to Russia's Soviet fleet, is also based in the area.

A tumult ensued when the pro-Western President of Ukraine, Viktor Yuschenko, proclaimed that it is only allowed to stay in the key port until 2017. Immediately after pro-Russian President Viktor Yanukovych held office in 2010, he approved the extension of the Russian tenancy until 2042 in exchange for Russian gas supply discounts. In March, Russia feared that Ukraine's new pro-Western administration will expel it, urging President Putin to send military troops to Crimea to 'defend' its base.

Made in the USA
Middletown, DE
10 July 2015